SCHOOLS COUNCIL RESEARCH STUDIES

Entry and performance at Oxford and Cambridge 1966–71

ALSO IN SCHOOLS COUNCIL RESEARCH STUDIES

The Universities and the Sixth Form Curriculum
by W. A. Reid
A first report from a Schools Council project
on the sixth form curriculum and examinations
(Macmillan Education, 1972)

OTHER SCHOOLS COUNCIL RESEARCH PUBLICATIONS

Enquiry 1: Young School Leavers
A report of a survey among young people, parents
and teachers carried out for the Schools Council
by the Government Social Survey (HMSO, 1968)

i.t.a.: An Independent Evaluation
by F. W. Warburton and Vera Southgate
The report of a study carried out for the Schools
Council on the use of the initial teaching
alphabet as a medium for beginning reading
with infants (John Murray/W. & R. Chambers, 1969)

i.t.a.: What is the Evidence?
by Vera Southgate
This short digest presents a selection of
those findings of general interest to parents
and teachers (John Murray/W. & R. Chambers, 1970)

Schools Council Sixth Form Survey
Volume I: Sixth Form Pupils and Teachers
A report of Phase I of a survey carried out for
the Schools Council by the Government Social Survey
(Councils & Education Press for Books for Schools, 1970)

Volume II: Students in Full-time Courses in Colleges
of Further Education
A report of Phase IIA of a survey carried out for
the Schools Council by the Government Social Survey
(Councils & Education Press for Books for Schools, 1970)

Volume III: Sixth Form Leavers
A report of Phase IIB of a survey carried out for
the Schools Council by the Government Social Survey
(Councils & Education Press for Books for Schools, 1971)

SCHOOLS COUNCIL RESEARCH STUDIES

Entry and performance at Oxford and Cambridge 1966–71

SIR DESMOND LEE

A report from the Schools Council project on Sixth Form Curricula and the Academic Requirements of Oxford and Cambridge, based at University College, Cambridge

DISTRIBUTED BY MACMILLAN
FOR THE SCHOOLS COUNCIL

Distributed for the Schools Council by
Macmillan Education Ltd
Houndmills, Basingstoke, Hampshire

SBN 333 14586 0

First published 1972 by the Schools Council
160 Great Portland Street, London W1N 6LL

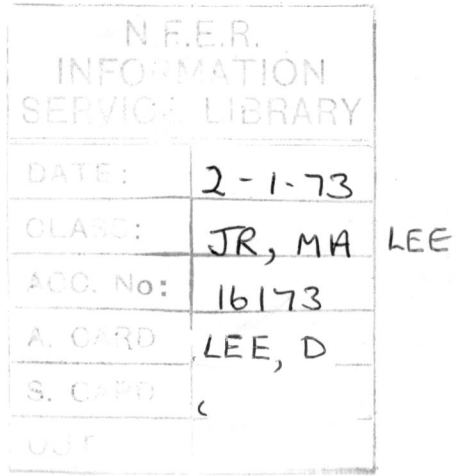
 PRINTED BY Unwin Brothers Limited
THE GRESHAM PRESS OLD WOKING SURREY ENGLAND

Produced by 'Uneoprint'

A member of the Staples Printing Group   (G4504)

Contents

Tables

6

Acknowledgements

This report has only been made possible by the kindness and patience of many people both at Oxford and Cambridge. Thanks are due especially to the Admissions Office at Oxford and the Intercollegiate Applications Office at Cambridge, without which the statistical basis of the material would not have existed. To their Secretaries, E. A. Baskerville and Miss C. V. Bevan, a particular debt of gratitude is owed for their constant helpfulness. At Cambridge thanks are due also to the Student Records Section of the Registry, and in particular to D. J. H. Murphy, Assistant Registrary, and to Dennis Barrington-Light, University Computer Officer. I am grateful also to those at both universities who were kind enough to read and comment on the text in draft: it owes much to their judgement and encouragement. Finally, I should like to say how much the study owes to my Research Assistant Miss Angela Goldman, to her clarity of mind and her unruffled mathematical skill.

For any opinions expressed in the report and for errors remaining the responsibility is entirely mine. It is perhaps hardly necessary to add that no responsibility attaches to the Schools Council, to whom I am grateful for giving me the opportunity to do the work, as I am also to the President and Fellows of University College for initiating the project and electing me to a Senior Research Fellowship.

Desmond Lee

Author's preface

The text which follows is the outcome of a project sponsored at University College, Cambridge, by the Schools Council with the purpose of examining some of the problems posed to schools and their sixth forms by the entry requirements of Oxford and Cambridge. Many of those problems were considered by a Working Party on the Cambridge Colleges' Joint Examination, of which I was fortunate enough to be a member, and to whose two reports reference is particularly made in Chapter 2 of what follows. But it was also part of the project's purpose to collect, clarify and in some respects amplify information available about the entry to the two universities. Inevitably, much of this work took a statistical form, and statistics are to most people indigestible material. As a friend and one-time colleague said to me, 'When are you going to tell us what all these figures you keep producing are about?' I have tried in this report to bear his question in mind, to present the statistical material in a manageable form, and to set it against the background of a brief account of admissions procedure and the college examinations. There is a danger that to some the result will seem too elementary, to others still allusively obscure. But at least I hope that readers will find many of the relevant facts about the entry to the two universities set out with reasonable clarity, and some new interest in the record of the performance of those admitted. I and other members of the project team are well aware of the limitations of what we have done; we have not always, for example, been able to deal with the special features of the women's entry as fully as we could have wished. But we hope that within those limitations the report will prove relevant and useful, not least to the wide range of schools making application to the two universities, both of which would like to extend the range still further.

1 Admissions procedure and requirements

Admissions procedure

The procedure for admission to Oxford and Cambridge is not uncommonly regarded as being both complicated and mysterious. Much of the mystery disappears when a few basic principles are understood, and explanation of them can well start by contrasting the system which obtains at these two universities, by which the colleges control admissions, and the system of admission by university faculty or (more commonly) department, which is the normal procedure at other British universities. The greatest part of the entry each year consists of admissions from school to read a first degree course; and the study which follows is concerned solely with such admissions and takes no account of those doing postgraduate work or of graduates admitted with Senior (Oxford) or Affiliated (Cambridge) status to read first degree courses. Inevitable cross-classifications make it difficult to give precise figures of undergraduates (so defined) and post-graduate students, but in round figures undergraduate numbers at Oxford in the academic year 1970/71 were men 6350, women 1530; at Cambridge men 7100, women 1065. The corresponding figures for graduates (full-time) were 2590 and 450 at Oxford, 2155 and 400 at Cambridge.

In virtually all universities in the United Kingdom, admission to read for first degrees is, as has been said, the responsibility of the department. This responsibility may have been delegated, but the department and its admissions officer enjoy almost complete autonomy in the admissions process, the admissions officer himself (usually a lecturer or a senior lecturer) having very wide discretion. There is little central oversight of admissions policies by the university; as Sir Eric Ashby has remarked, in this as in other matters policy is not dictated from above and there is no descending chain of authority. Anyone who has attended discussions with vice-chancellors about entry requirements must have been conscious that behind them stood faculty and department, which would make the final decision. This dominance of the department in the admissions process (which, it may be noted in passing, is uncommon outside the United Kingdom) facilitates coherent policy on admissions within a department, but it means that admissions are made primarily with departmental purposes in view; this produces the overall complexity of special requirements set out in *A Compendium of University Entrance Requirements*, compiled by the Committee of Vice-Chancellors and Principals of the Universities of the United Kingdom. (See References, p. 46, under Ashby and Reid.)

In contrast with this, at Oxford and Cambridge the sole authority for admission to first degree courses is the college. Candidates must fulfil the basic university matriculation requirements (which pose no great problem) but there are no faculty requirements and it is the colleges who determine the requirements to be made of entrants. Each college has one admissions officer or more, commonly known as the admissions tutor. Colleges vary in the amount of discretion they allow to their admissions tutor or tutors; it is likely to be wider at Cambridge than at Oxford. But all deal directly with candidates, in consultation with the subject tutors or directors of studies who will ultimately be supervising them, and are responsible for admitting to the college a cross-section of entrants to all faculties and departments in which the college is prepared to arrange tuition (and exceptions will be few). The balance of numbers between faculties and departments at university level, though it is the subject of some anxiety, has been achieved not by restricting the activities of the colleges (though occasionally there have been quotas for particular faculties) but because the pattern of recruitment which particular colleges follow remains fairly consistent from year to year. Colleges have to arrange for the individual teaching of undergraduates, and in practice therefore admit similar numbers to read the different subjects each year. University control of the process operates indirectly rather than directly, in that the candidates admitted will have to take and pass examinations set by the university authorities, and colleges determine their standards with reference to those examinations. Admissions tutors are looking for academic success, not failure.

Admissions tutors, therefore (though normally involved in faculty work and in teaching), are not directly influenced by faculty or departmental considerations in making their selection. The academic criteria which they use are GCE A level and the colleges' examinations. The majority of candidates for the men's colleges have already passed GCE A level, and though some may be given admission on the results they have obtained, the main function of GCE for them, in general terms, is that of pre-selection by determining the field of the colleges' examinations, which all candidates at Oxford and the great majority of candidates at Cambridge must take to secure final acceptance. Much, perhaps most, of the work of pre-selection is done by the schools, who know the level of GCE performance needed in practice (see Tables 1 and 2, pp. 15 and 16) and discourage candidates unlikely to reach it. In addition to these academic criteria, there is a personal assessment based on school testimonial and interview. Though not every applicant is necessarily interviewed, it is in general true that all candidates finally admitted are interviewed, and some personal assessment is made of them on the basis of interview and testimonial. This policy of interview differs from that of other universities, where the purpose of interviews is a great deal more varied and both recruiting and administrative considerations are likely to be dominant.

The dangers of the Oxford and Cambridge system are that similarly qualified candidates may receive different treatment from different colleges (though efforts are made to avoid this), and that varying practice of the colleges may be difficult for schools to follow. The advantages of the procedure are that it is not dominated by departmental considerations and that it makes possible an individual treatment, looking forward to the system of individual teaching by tutorial and supervision which is characteristic of the two universities.

12

Relations with UCCA

Applicants to Oxford and Cambridge, as to other universities, must enter through the Universities Central Council on Admissions, and after the college examinations held in November/December the process of selection must be completed by 31 January. The main links between the universities and UCCA are the Admissions Office at Oxford and the Intercollegiate Applications Office at Cambridge. Though much of the work done by the two offices is similar, their status and procedure differ somewhat. Both universities require a special admission form of their own to be completed in addition to the UCCA form. At Oxford only one form is needed for all purposes, including that of entrance for the examination, and all forms are sent to the Admissions Office, which then distributes them to colleges. At Cambridge candidates must complete a preliminary application form, a card for record purposes for the Applications Office and entry cards for the examination (there are separate cards and instructions for each group); all forms are then forwarded to the college of first preference. This procedure at Cambridge springs from the colleges' desire for direct contact with schools, but it is undoubtedly more complex than that of Oxford and it seems doubtful whether the direct contact, which both school and university would agree to be desirable, is facilitated by complexities of procedure. The Cambridge Applications Office has a link with the Student Record Section of the University Registry, which has considerable advantages, including the use of the Old Schools Computer for statistical purposes.

Academic qualifications

Candidates qualify for admission, as indicated above, by securing passes in appropriate subjects and levels of pass in GCE, and the great majority of them by also taking the colleges' examinations—called at Oxford the College Entrance and Scholarship Examination, at Cambridge the Colleges' Joint Examination—or the examinations of the women's colleges. The only formal requirement made by the university is matriculation; in their further selection, colleges are guided both by GCE performance and by the results of their own examinations.

Matriculation

The normal way of satisfying matriculation requirements is by suitable passes in GCE. Though some candidates may still have to complete matriculation requirements after acceptance, this does not normally present great difficulty. The requirements of the two universities vary in detail but their common ground may be briefly described as follows:

(a)   a pass in use of English or an approved alternative;

(b)   four passes in GCE, of which two must be at A level: one of the four must be a mathematics or science subject, and one must be a foreign language.

13

College admissions

The use made of GCE for admissions purposes varies between the universities and colleges. The women's colleges rely largely on their own examinations (but see p. 20 on pre- and post-A level candidates). At the men's colleges its main purpose, as indicated above, is pre-selection, since at both universities a high proportion of candidates for admission have already taken A levels. At Oxford a small number of places may be given on the strength of GCE results (plus school report and interview) but practically all candidates take the entrance and scholarship examination. At Cambridge the position is more complicated. Some candidates are given definite acceptance on A level results and are not required to take any further examination, but the majority of candidates so accepted are encouraged or required to take the Colleges' Joint Examination. Candidates taking that examination for admissions purposes only and not for award may be asked to take a limited number of papers in it; the requirements of groups and of individual colleges vary. Any candidate may enter for an award, but candidates applying for admission only may be refused permission to sit for the examination on the results of their A levels. In practice, a great majority of candidates, whether for admission or award, take the Cambridge examination; in 1970 (for entry in 1971) 4196 out of 5064 did so.

In their examination, both universities provide for candidates who have not yet taken A level by setting special questions in some subjects. At Cambridge a small percentage of candidates (at present about 25%) may obtain acceptance conditional upon A levels to be obtained in the following summer, though college practice in the matter varies, as a recent article in *HMA Review* (July 1971) has shown. Under the universities' agreement with UCCA, such candidates may not be examined by the colleges.

One other feature of the Oxford and Cambridge entry may be noted here. Well over half the candidates for admission, and a higher proportion of those accepted, have taken S level papers and admissions tutors give considerable weight to S level papers in assessing candidates' GCE performance. The figures for 1971 were:

Percentages of candidates with distinction or merit on S level papers

	APPLICATIONS		ACCEPTANCES	
	Men (%)	Women (%)	Men (%)	Women (%)
Oxford	53	49	67	54
Cambridge	58	49	71	69

Standards

GCE results thus play a large part in the admission process, mainly by determining the field from which selection is made. There is of course no formal regulation or agreement about the standards required, but on the basis of admissions and other statistics it is possible to give some indication of the standards actually reached by those finally admitted. Table 1

14

shows the proportion of candidates in the three UCCA grades (see p. 45) applying to and accepted by Oxford and Cambridge, compared with the proportion at all other universities as shown in the UCCA 1970 sample.

Table 1 Percentages of university applications and acceptances: by GCE score

GCE score (see p. 45)	Applications			Acceptances		
	UCCA sample, 1970	Oxford, 1971	Cambridge, 1971	UCCA sample, 1970	Oxford, 1971	Cambridge, 1971
	%	%	%	%	%	%
MEN						
Three A levels						
15-13	20	40	54	25	60	70
12-9	38	40	35	45	35	25
8-3	42	20	11	30	6	3
TOTALS*	100	100	100	100	100	100
Two A levels						
10-9	4	18	28	12	42	49
8-5	40	44	42	50	47	34
4-2	56	38	31	38	11	17
TOTALS*	100	100	100	100	100	100
WOMEN						
Three A levels						
15-13	21	51	54	26	64	73
12-9	43	38	35	50	29	24
8-3	36	11	11	24	7	4
TOTALS*	100	100	100	100	100	100
Two A levels						
10-9	7	23	33	17	47	60
8-5	51	46	35	67	37	30
4-2	42	31	32	16	16	10
TOTALS*	100	100	100	100	100	100

* In this and subsequent tables, percentages have been rounded and so do not always add up to exactly 100.

The level of achievement expected varies between different subjects, being in general higher in sciences and mathematics than in arts subjects. This may in part account for the slightly higher proportion of high UCCA grades in the Cambridge entry. Some indication of the distribution of GCE achievement between different subjects is given in Table 2, which analyses in terms of GCE score the entry in nine major subjects from the 1966 admission.

Table 2 Percentages of candidates with three A levels reaching a given A level performance (1966 entry): men candidates in Oxford Finals and Cambridge Tripos Part I in the subjects named (cumulative percentages)

OXFORD   CAMBRIDGE

	GCE score					GCE score			
	15	14	13	$\leqslant$12		15	14	13	$\leqslant$12
	%	%	%	%		%	%	%	%
Chemistry	24	52	72	100	Nat. sciences	51	74	87	100
Classics									
(Greats)	21	41	60	100	Classics	14	40	59	100
English	15	23	39	100	English	13	33	48	100
History	12	26	34	100	History	9	26	48	100
Jurisprudence	6	24	34	100	Law	11	23	43	100
Mathematics	31	52	68	100	Mathematics	67	89	96	100
Mod. languages	22	41	55	100	Mod. languages	23	45	60	100
Physics	30	58	78	100	Engineering	41	68	82	100
PPE	15	31	46	100	Economics	10	26	41	100

Figures are available for a rather larger range of scores at Cambridge and show that, of the nine subjects, five have percentages of more than 90 with a score of ten or more; three have percentages of more than 80; and that in only one subject is the percentage less than 80. The distribution of candidates between the GCE boards is dealt with on p. 26.

2 The Oxford College Entrance and Scholarship Examination and the Cambridge Colleges' Joint Examination (OES and CJE)

History

Neither of the examinations for the men's colleges is so much a carefully and deliberately thought-out system as a product of a particular historical development. Both were originally examinations for awards, which provided financial assistance for able boys. Between the wars £100 per annum (the typical maximum award) provided a much higher proportion of the cost of fees and residence than it would today.

The colleges originally examined independently, but between the wars formed themselves into groups, the process taking a rather different course at the two universities. At Oxford groups of colleges were formed first on a subject basis, with two or three groups offering scholarships in each subject, classics or modern languages and so on. In addition, there were examinations at three dates, December, January and March, and the different subject groups were rotated between those dates in such a way that there was a choice of subjects at each date, with different colleges examining in different subjects at a different date each year. The large number of Oxford closed or restricted awards fell outside this system, many being examined for in October or November. Schools liked the three dates of examination on the whole, as they felt that their candidates had more than one chance of award (though the number of awards available was unaffected by the number of chances). Under this system scholarships were tied to subjects, and a college which did not fill its awards in one subject could not transfer them to another.

At Cambridge three groups were eventually formed in the 1930s; all three examined in December and all subjects were examined at once. (Two colleges remained outside this grouping and examined in March until 1960.) Awards were not tied to subjects, so that the advertised awards could be distributed among subjects according to the strength of the field in each. For the conduct of the examination each group appointed a panel of examiners, who set the papers and conducted the examination, co-opting additional examiners if necessary. The examiners recommended candidates for major or minor scholarship or for exhibition, and their recommendations were final in the sense that no college was allowed to make an award which had not been recommended by the examiners. This method of examination contrasts with that at Oxford, where (though practice was never entirely uniform) each college generally examined and considered its own field of candidates separately and elected from it if satisfied, but could consider rejects from other colleges in the group if not.

Though the primary purpose of the examination at both universities was the allocation of awards, colleges which required some further test before admission in addition to matriculation could give commoner admission to candidates who did not obtain an award. But many colleges which wanted such a test held a separate special examination for commoners; such examinations were run by individual colleges.

Present arrangements

The present arrangements for examination are a development of this system. Since the war there has been increasing pressure on the entry, and the use of the examinations for entry purposes at Oxford and Cambridge has become more and more common until it is now almost universal, a fact which is reflected in the present titles of the two examinations. In 1962 Oxford set up a committee of enquiry which recommended a single examination for all admissions to the men's colleges; and when the two universities entered the UCCA scheme in 1965, there were certain further consequential changes in the earlier system. At Oxford scholarships remain linked to subjects, but the January and March examinations have disappeared, and examinations are held by all groups in all subjects at the end of November, when Cambridge also examines.

At both universities the group system continues for administrative and examining purposes, and for entry and distribution of candidates. A single set of papers is now set in each subject and is common to all groups, whereas previously each group set its own papers. The arrangements described above for the conduct of the examination at each university continue, except that in mathematics at Oxford and geography and music at Cambridge a single panel of examiners deals with candidates from all groups. But the effect is that the colleges at both universities are conducting what is increasingly a single examination. Candidates express a preference between colleges in the group and may be taken by colleges of their second or later preference within the group if their first choice has no place for them; there is also an inter-group and inter-university pool which perform the same function at later stages. But the great majority of candidates (about 90%) are taken by their colleges of first preference, with rather greater interchange at Oxford than at Cambridge.

The increasing unity of the examination has been recognized at Oxford by the constitution of a single management committee and a unified entry procedure through the Admissions Office. At Cambridge the Executive Committee of the Tutors has now assumed overall control of the examination, and there is a Secretary of the CJE to deal with common administrative arrangements; but each group has its own entry forms for the examination, which are sent in through the individual college, and the Applications Office has no part in the administration of the examination (an arrangement which schools often find confusing).

The examinations and the schools

Nearly 800 schools sent men applicants for the 1971 admission to Oxford, over 1000 to Cambridge. As the great majority of applicants take the examinations, their influence among schools must be considerable. Close contact between schools and colleges is therefore essential. Colleges try to ensure this partly by informal means, e.g. correspondence, visits, the appointment of schoolmaster fellows. But there are also regular conferences (held by colleges both individually and jointly), and comments on papers set in each year's examination are sent in through the Joint Four.[*] But still closer contact might be possible within the field of individual subjects. There are no defined subject-syllabuses, though many examiners have experience of A level, and A level syllabuses are borne in mind; but further measures seem desirable. The Working Party on the Cambridge Colleges' Joint Examination suggested in its *First Report* (1970) that for each subject there should be a standing committee, with Chairman and Secretary, and that the examiners should consult schoolmasters and representatives of examining boards as assessors. It recommended also that there should be a standing joint committee between Oxford and Cambridge on the two examinations. To many schools Oxford and Cambridge present a single problem, and though complete uniformity may be undesirable, any reduction in unnecessary differences would be welcomed by them. And a system of subject committees would give a coherent frame of reference and continuity, and make consultation with schools and boards easier. It should be added that elements of this structure already exist. Subject committees are being formed at Cambridge, and schoolmaster assessors have been used at both universities.

Two comments may be made in conclusion. In the first place, though the Cambridge Working Party suggested that entrance awards should be abandoned, that view has not been accepted by either the Cambridge or the Oxford colleges as a whole. This means that the problem of providing for both the award winner and the commoner, including the pre-A level candidate, remains. To some this seems a difficult problem. But as noted above (p. 14), provision is already made for the pre-A level candidate, and the women's colleges have always used a single examination for both purposes. Perhaps a pattern in which candidates for award took extra papers or questions, on the lines of GCE A and S levels, would provide a better solution—a suggestion made in the *Second Report* of the Cambridge Working Party (1971). Schools which can only offer a two-year sixth form course certainly feel that every effort should be made to give their candidates as fair a chance of entry as possible.

In the second place, neither university is at present inclined to discontinue its examination, whatever its particular form may be. There are those who consider that the examinations duplicate effort both for examiners and candidates (the arguments are fully rehearsed in the Cambridge Working Party's *First Report*). But the colleges have to pick from a well-qualified field, and need some means of doing so. In addition, there are likely to be changes in the public examination system at both O and A level in the comparatively near future, so that from the point of view both of the schools and of the universities, an element of stability may be an advantage. This could be provided by the OES and CJE, especially if the measures for consultation here suggested, both between the two universities and with schools, are adopted.

---

[*] The Headmasters' Association, the Association of Headmistresses, the Assistant Masters' Association and the Association of Assistant Mistresses.

The women's colleges: pre- and post-A level candidates

The women's colleges have always examined separately from the mens', and in the past so arranged the dates of their examinations that candidates could take the examination for the women's colleges of both Oxford and Cambridge. (New Hall makes no entrance awards and requires examination in certain subjects only.) In future the women's colleges at both universities will examine at the same time, and will be joined for purposes of the entry of women by the mixed colleges at Cambridge, where the women's and mixed colleges will form a single group for the entry of women. It would be premature to comment at this stage on the proposed arrangements for examination and for the operation of candidates' preference lists. But the requirement that candidates for either university must take a paper from the other university's examination, if they are to be considered by a college there, may perhaps be reconsidered in time; the new arrangement has given an opportunity to eliminate rather than emphasize differences. And it is to be hoped that within each university the use of the same examination papers for men and women, which has just begun, will rapidly become general. Boys and girls take the same GCE papers, and many come from mixed schools which may send candidates of both sexes to mixed colleges.

There are, of course, some significant differences between the men's and the women's entry, since there are fewer places available for women and a different proportion of places to candidates, as well as differences between boys' schools and girls' schools. There are fewer large sixth forms in girls' schools (Table 5, p. 23—though the pattern of greater success for larger sixth forms is the same in both types of school) and, no doubt in consequence, the proportion of girls staying for a third year or part of a third year in the sixth form is lower. This last point is illustrated by the different numbers of pre- and post-A level candidates and acceptances (1971 entry). A post-A level candidate is defined for this purpose as one who had passed two or more A levels by October 1970.

	Men		Women	
	Applications	Acceptances	Applications	Acceptances
Oxford				
Post-A level	2663	1416	771	288
Pre-A level	1188	456	1004	222
Cambridge				
Post-A level	3286	1840	785	204
Pre-A level	1674	629	1011	158

At the men's colleges the proportion of pre-A level candidates so defined (the great majority of whom will be taking a two-year course in the sixth form) is about 25% of those finally admitted, at the women's colleges 40-45%.

3 Description of the entry

The preceding chapters, with their very brief account of admission procedure and examinations, are intended as an introduction and background to
the next two, which give a statistical description, under various headings,
of the entry to the two universities, and an analysis of the performance in
university examinations of those admitted. The sources of the information
summarized in these sections are given in the References (p. 46).

Type of school and size of sixth form

The Admissions and Applications Offices have classified schools under the
three main headings: *maintained, direct grant,* and *independent.* The classification has, directly or by implication, some descriptive value. But the
information which it gives is limited, being based on a criterion which,

Table 3 Percentages of candidates applying and accepted from each
type of school

Type of school	Men			Women		
	UCCA sample, 1970	Oxford, 1971	Cam-bridge, 1971	UCCA sample, 1970	Oxford, 1971	Cam-bridge, 1971
Applications	%	%	%	%	%	%
Maintained	61	45	44	61	48	46
Direct grant	8	15	15	10	21	19
Independent	12	36	32	9	24	24
Scottish and Irish	10	2	4	13	1	2
Other	9	2	5	7	6	9
TOTALS	100	100	100	100	100	100
Total numbers	—	3851	5064	—	1775	1854
Acceptances	%	%	%	%	%	%
Maintained	61	42	40	63	40	41
Direct grant	9	17	17	12	29	29
Independent	13	38	36	8	27	24
Scottish and Irish	9	2	4	11	1	1
Other	8	1	4	6	3	5
TOTALS	100	100	100	100	100	100
Total numbers	—	1872	2500	—	510	368

Table 4 Numbers of schools sending applicants and gaining places; average numbers of candidates sent and successful (1971 entry): by type of school

| | Type of school | | | | | |
	Main- tained	Direct grant	Inde- pendent	Scottish & Irish	Other	TOTALS
NO. OF SCHOOLS						
Men						
Applications:						
Oxford	532	76	132	25	26	791
Cambridge	717	80	174	57	*	1028
Acceptances:						
Oxford	369	65	113	19	14	580
Cambridge	468	72	137	32	*	709
Women						
Applications:						
Oxford	413	79	124	17	24	657
Cambridge	435	75	148	24	*	682
Acceptances:						
Oxford	153	49	57	7	16	282
Cambridge	121	49	49	4	*	223
AVERAGE NO. OF CANDIDATES PER SCHOOL						
Men						
Applications:						
Oxford	3.3	7.7	10.3	2.4	3.4	4.9
Cambridge	3.1	9.5	9.3	3.3	*	4.9
Acceptances:						
Oxford	2.1	5.1	6.3	2.0	1.6	3.2
Cambridge	2.1	5.9	6.5	3.0	*	3.5
Women						
Applications:						
Oxford	2.0	4.8	3.4	1.6	4.6	2.7
Cambridge	1.9	4.7	3.0	1.4	*	2.7
Acceptances:						
Oxford	1.3	3.0	2.3	1.0	1.1	1.8
Cambridge	1.3	2.2	1.8	1.0	*	1.7

* Not available

though it may have educational implications, has no strict educational relevance. The degree of a school's dependence on public funds has no necessary relation to the type of education provided. It is clearly desirable to supplement the classification and to be able to say, for example, whether a school is comprehensive, grammar or sixth form college; whether it is mixed or single-sex, day or boarding; and (perhaps most important) what is the size of its sixth form. Much of this detail is difficult or impossible to obtain from published sources, but arrangements are in hand to obtain fuller information from the Department of Education and Science.

The present position under the threefold classification is shown in Tables 3 and 4. The proportion of acceptances from the three types of school corresponds closely to the proportion of applications, and has done so since the two offices started keeping records. Information about earlier years is scarce. But in the years before the war the entry from independent schools was between 60% and 70%, and from direct grant schools around 12%. In 1961 the combined figure for the two universities for the three types of school was: maintained 32%, direct grant 17%, independent 51%. The present figures have been fairly constant since 1965, though there has been a slight decrease in the independent school proportion and a slight increase in the maintained. Figures for the women's entry before application was made through the two offices in 1968 are not readily available, so change over the years cannot be numerically indicated, but again the patterns of application and acceptance are similar. The most notable feature of the women's entry is the high proportion of success of the direct grant schools—a feature also notable in the men's entry but not to the same extent.

The number of schools submitting candidates has remained fairly constant at Oxford, though there has been a slight increase; at Cambridge

Table 5 Sixth form sizes of Cambridge 1966 entrants' schools in England and Wales compared with sixth form sizes (at January 1968) of all schools in England and Wales

Sixth form size	Boys' schools		Mixed schools		Girls' schools	
	Cambridge	All	Cambridge	All	Cambridge	All
1-90:						
no. of schools	73	402	37	971	35	665
%	17	46	22	71	23	64
91-120:						
no. of schools	57	133	34	155	37	180
%	14	15	20	11	25	18
121-150:						
no. of schools	104	133	33	100	32	98
%	25	15	20	7	21	10
151-210:						
no. of schools	106	138	40	108	39	57
%	25	16	24	8	26	6
211 and over:						
no. of schools	80	79	22	37	7	10
%	19	9	13	3	5	1
TOTALS:						
no. of schools	420	885	166	1371	150	1010
%	100	100	100	100	100	100

the increase is rather larger, and has taken place almost entirely in the maintained sector (the 1965 figure was 631). The direct grant and independent groups each send more candidates per school than the maintained. This may be a function of sixth form size, as many of them have large sixth forms.

Although, as already noted, it is not possible to obtain information about sixth form size from published sources, this information was secured from the great majority (736 in all) of schools represented in the 1966 Cambridge entry. Figures for all schools were supplied by the Department of Education and Science. The result is shown in Table 5 (see also p. 43).

It seems unlikely that the Oxford entry would yield a very different result. The noticeable feature of the table is the high proportion of Cambridge entrants who come from the larger sixth forms. Though many smaller sixth forms are admirable, the larger unit can give a wide choice of subject and subject combination, can attract highly qualified teachers, and is likely to be able to make it easier for pupils to reach the standards of achievement which the two universities demand.

Table 6 Percentages of applications and acceptances of candidates (1971 entry): by geographical region of school

Region of school	Applications Oxford %	Applications Cambridge %	Acceptances Oxford %	Acceptances Cambridge %	All GCE sixth formers, 1969 %
Men					
North	3	3	3	3	6
Northwest	12	10	12	11	13
Yorks & Humberside	5	7	8	7	9
East Midlands	6	7	6	7	7
West Midlands	9	9	11	9	9
East Anglia	2	4	1	5	3
Greater London	14	17	14	17	16
Other Southeast	33	29	32	29	22
Southwest	12	10	11	9	9
Wales	4	4	3	3	6
TOTALS	100	100	100	100	100
Women					
North	4	4	3	6	7
Northwest	9	8	8	9	13
Yorks & Humberside	7	7	9	5	10
East Midlands	7	5	5	5	6
West Midlands	7	7	6	8	9
East Anglia	5	5	5	6	2
Greater London	19	20	20	22	16
Other Southeast	26	27	26	28	21
Southwest	12	12	14	10	9
Wales	4	3	2	2	7
TOTALS	100	100	100	100	100

Geographical distribution and social class

Tables 6 and 7 show the entry analysed by geographical region of school and by occupation of parent respectively. In the geographical table the percentage in each region of sixth formers taking GCE A level courses is given for comparison, since they constitute the effective pool of candidates and are a better standard of comparison than the total number of 18-year-olds, used by UCCA in its similar table. In the table showing parental occupation the classification is that used by UCCA. The UCCA forms do not give enough information to make possible the fuller classification used by the Registrar-General.

The two universities admit noticeably less than their proportionate share from the North and Wales; but the deterrent of distance and regional attraction make that not altogether surprising. Otherwise the pattern of admissions follows very closely the pattern of the available pool, with the Southeast making up for deficiencies from other regions (the deficiencies from North, Northwest and Wales are almost exactly balanced by the higher figure for the Southeast). The amount of information available about the social class of university entrants in general is limited and the classifica-

Table 7 Percentages of applications and acceptances: by occupation of parent

Occupation of parent	Applications			Acceptances		
	UCCA sample, 1970 %	Oxford, 1971 %	Cam- bridge, 1971 %	UCCA sample, 1970 %	Oxford, 1971 %	Cam- bridge, 1971 %
Men						
Administrators & managers	13	17	17	13	18	18
Professional, technical, etc.	25	35	38	27	37	40
Other non-manual	26	24	24	25	25	23
Manual & agricultural	27	16	15	28	14	14
Unidentified	9	7	6	7	5	6
TOTALS	100	100	100	100	100	100
Women						
Administrators & managers	13	17	17	14	17	17
Professional, technical, etc.	30	42	47	31	46	50
Other non-manual	25	22	22	25	22	20
Manual & agricultural	24	13	10	23	11	11
Unidentified	8	6	4	7	3	2
TOTALS	100	100	100	100	100	100

tions used are often not comparable. Table 7 gives some reasonably reliable, if restricted, information. It will be noticed that again the pattern of acceptance closely follows the pattern of application to the two universities.

Analysis by GCE examining boards and type of subject to be read

Table 8 shows the distribution of the entry between the GCE examining boards by percentage and by numbers. In the men's entry, the high proportion of applications and entrants from the Oxford and Cambridge Joint Board has often been noticed. It is simple to account for it. The Board has a large number of independent and direct grant establishments among the schools which it examines, and these two types of school between them supply nearly half the entry (see Table 3, p. 21). Of the 1967 entrants, 88% of those from independent schools and 37% of those from direct grant schools had taken the Oxford and Cambridge Joint Board's examination. The high proportion of entrants from the Board is a natural consequence, although it appears to have declined slightly in the last five years, from about 48% in 1966 to 45% in 1970. The balance of direct grant entrants

Table 8 Numbers and percentages of applications and acceptances (1971 entry): by GCE examining board

GCE examining board	Applications				Acceptances			
	Oxford No.	%	Cambridge No.	%	Oxford No.	%	Cambridge No.	%
Men								
O & C	1590	42	1972	40	834	45	1092	45
C	368	9	667	14	172	10	312	13
O	424	11	455	9	175	10	216	9
L	448	12	674	14	188	10	275	11
JMB	799	21	938	19	413	22	463	19
Other	180	5	178	4	64	4	73	3
TOTALS	3809	100	4884	100	1846	100	2431	100
Women								
O & C	77	5	70	4	27	7	17	5
C	312	18	357	20	96	19	83	23
O	326	19	322	18	82	16	55	15
L	539	31	593	34	161	32	125	34
JMB	401	23	357	20	120	24	75	21
Other	73	4	62	4	11	2	7	2
TOTALS	1728	100	1761	100	497	100	362	100

Key: O & C Oxford and Cambridge Joint Board
   C Cambridge
   O Oxford
   L London
  JMB Joint Matriculation Board

come in the main from the Joint Matriculation Board (42%). Fifty per cent of maintained school entrants come from the London or Joint Matriculation Boards, about half from each, and another 45% from the Oxford and Cambridge Joint, Oxford and Cambridge Boards in about equal proportions.

The majority of women entrants come from the London, Joint Matriculation, Oxford or Cambridge Boards, London usually having the highest proportion. The Oxford and Cambridge Joint Board examines very few women candidates (less than 700).

In terms of achievement, women entrants with three A levels and high scores (13-15) are fairly evenly distributed between boards. The Oxford and Joint Matriculation Boards provide the highest percentage of men with high scores in three A levels (though the Oxford Board's numbers are comparatively small), the Oxford and Cambridge Joint Board the lowest (percentages in UCCA Grade I (see p. 45) were: Oxford 82%, Joint Matriculation Board 80% Oxford and Cambridge Joint Board 59% for 1967, and comparable for 1966). Conversely, the Oxford and Cambridge Joint Board has a higher proportion of those with lower GCE scores in the range accepted, which reflects the higher proportion of candidates with such scores who apply from the independent schools which constitute a large part of the Board's field. But the proportion from any board with scores of 9 or below was small (10% or less).

Table 9 shows the distribution of candidates between three main types of subject. A higher proportion of men read arts and social science than sciences at Oxford; at Cambridge the balance is about equal, with sciences, including the large engineering faculty, having a slight preponderance. At both universities the majority of women read arts or social science, and any increase in the number of women would presumably lead to an increase in the proportion in the faculties concerned.

Table 9 Percentages of arts, social science, and sciences applications and acceptances (1971 entry)

Subject type	Men		Women	
	Oxford %	Cambridge %	Oxford %	Cambridge %
Applications				
Arts	35 ⎰ 55	33 ⎰ 50	55 ⎰ 67	54 ⎰ 64
Social science	20 ⎱	17 ⎱	12 ⎱	10 ⎱
Sciences	45	51	33	36
TOTALS	100	100	100	100
Acceptances				
Arts	39 ⎰ 58	33 ⎰ 49	55 ⎰ 68	56 ⎰ 63
Social science	19 ⎱	16 ⎱	13 ⎱	7 ⎱
Sciences	42	51	32	38
TOTALS	100	100	100	100

The field of recruitment

It is sometimes asked whether the field from which the two universities recruit is as wide as it could or should be. Before answering this question, it is necessary to know how wide the present field is. And this further question is in turn not easy to answer, though some indications can be gleaned from the information presented in this chapter. It is best considered from two points of view: that of the number of schools presenting candidates, and that of the level of achievement which candidates are expected to reach.

It is impossible, on present information, to find out how great an overlap there is between the schools applying to Oxford and to Cambridge: if over 800 schools (in round figures) sent applicants to Oxford for the men's entry in 1971 and over 1000 to Cambridge, what is the total number of schools applying to the two universities? There is the same problem with the women's entry, and the additional complication that many mixed schools send in candidates, and may therefore be included not only in the total for each university but also for both men and women. When enquiries were being made about sixth forms for the purpose of Table 5 it appeared that about 1700 schools (boys, girls and mixed) had made application to Cambridge at some time during the previous five years. Information at the Oxford Admissions Office suggests a total at least as great. The overlap between Cambridge and Oxford must be large, but it seems a fair estimate to say that some 2000 schools are included in the field from which the two universities recruit, though doubtless many do not send candidates regularly or in large numbers. For comparison, the number of schools on the UCCA mailing list, used by the two offices, is between three and four thousand. It comprises a wide range of secondary schools, and some further definition can be obtained from the DES *Statistics of Education, 1969*. These give a total of some 2500 maintained grammar, comprehensive, technical and similar secondary schools, 182 direct grant and 693 independent secondary. Most of the direct grant schools send candidates, and some 350 of the independent schools. The remaining independent schools are unlikely to provide much of a field for further recruitment, and so it would appear that the present field covers a large proportion of those schools which are a likely source of applicants.

This leads to consideration of the level of achievement. So long as the two universities require a standard of achievement such as that shown in Tables 1 and 2 (pp. 15 and 16) there will be a large number of candidates who think (rightly) that they have little chance of success if they apply, and there will be schools which produce few candidates who reach the standard and which therefore regard Oxford and Cambridge as outside their purview. The standard demanded, in short, inevitably curtails the field, which will be drawn largely from the more effective and larger sixth forms, especially those offering third-year sixth form work. The heads of most boys' schools and many mixed schools with such sixth forms are members of the Headmasters' Association. In 1971 this had a total of 1841 members, of which some 1600 were heads of grammar, comprehensive, technical, sixth form college, etc.; it has been calculated that of a national total of 144 000 boys in sixth forms 130 000 were in schools whose heads were members of the Association. Of the heads who successfully submitted applicants to Cambridge for 1966 nearly 90% were members. There is no reason to suppose that the figure for Oxford would be significantly different, and it would therefore appear that both universities draw widely on the most likely source of supply.

It is more difficult to generalize about the entry to the women's colleges, as the number of places available is so much smaller. But what has been said about standard of achievement must apply to them: the achievement of their entry in terms of A level is in fact higher than that of the men's (Table 1, p. 15).

In conclusion, it is worth recording that Dr J.W. Ashley Smith, writing in the *HMA Review* (December 1969) on the basis of figures now published in the two universities' Statistics of Admissions and asking the question 'Is there any sizeable field of untapped ability?' came to the conclusion that there was not.

4 Entrance awards

The examinations for entrance and awards have been described in Chapter
2, and the performance of award-holders will be dealt with in Chapter 5
and can be allowed to speak for itself. In Chapter 3 award-holders were
not distinguished from the rest of the entry, the terms of description covering all entrants without distinction. But the system of entrance awards is
a well-known and long-standing feature of the two universities which is
today the subject of some controversy; separate reference to it is required
in any account of the entry. No attempt will be made here to discuss the
controversial issues: they can be found in the *First Report* of the Working
Party on the Cambridge Colleges' Joint Examination. The object of what
follows will be to give a brief description of those features of the system
not mentioned elsewhere in this report.

The number of awards has increased considerably since 1950: in
round numbers from a total of about 800 in 1950 to over 1300 in 1968.
During the early years of the period, Cambridge gave rather more awards
than Oxford, but in the 1960s the position was reversed until in 1968, as a
result of a recommendation in the Franks Report (1966), the number of
open awards at Oxford was limited to one-third of the total admissions at any
college—which brought the Oxford figure down again very slightly below
that of Cambridge. The earlier distinction between different grades of
open entrance scholarship (typically between major and minor) has now
been abandoned, and open entrance awards fall into two categories: scholarships (usual value £60) and exhibitions (usual value £40). As a proportion
of the entry, if the distinction between open and restricted awards is
ignored, award-holders amounted to 36% at Oxford and 27% at Cambridge
in 1968.

There is a considerable difference between the two universities in the
number of restricted awards made each year. At Oxford the total is about
a hundred, at Cambridge about fifteen. Restricted awards have been much
criticized, and the Franks Report recommended their abolition. Two points
may be made about them here:

(a) As the Franks Report remarked, 'It can be said in general that all
winners of closed scholarships would certainly have got places and
would usually have won open awards.' Neither their standard nor their
attraction is low.
(b) The restriction is not always a narrow one. The limiting of a number
of Oxford awards to Wales or to Westmorland and Cumberland, for
example, is a restriction which offers an opportunity to a number of
schools and candidates, and an attraction in regions from which the
supply of candidates is low (see pp. 24-5).

There has been little change in the distribution of awards among the three types of school in the years since the war; the proportion won by the direct grant schools has increased slightly and that won by the independent has decreased. A typical recent distribution is given in Table 10. In 1953

Table 10 Distribution of awards among schools (1967 entry)

Type of school	Men				Women			
	Award-holders		Commoners		Award-holders		Commoners	
	No.	%	No.	%	No.	%	No.	%
Oxford								
Maintained	294	38	448	43	30	40	166	48
Direct grant	157	20	159	16	15	20	69	20
Independent	319	41	414	40	30	40	101	32
Other	4	1	13	1	—	—	4	—
TOTALS	774	100	1034	100	75	100	340	100
Cambridge								
Maintained	193	32	653	37	19	46	99	42
Direct grant	125	21	263	15	8	20	53	22
Independent	267	44	596	34	14	34	55	23
Other	20	3	263	15	—	—	30	13
TOTALS	605	100	1775	100	41	100	237	100

the combined figures for the two universities were: maintained 32%, direct grant 16%, independent 52%. It remains true, of course, that schools with large and effective sixth forms, and with experience of the examinations, are at an advantage in winning awards (as they are in winning places). In the period from 1964 to 1968, ten schools won between them some 15% of the awards made; and the schools winning awards most regularly are the independent and direct grant schools with strong sixth forms. But it would also be quite wrong to regard the winning of awards as the preserve of a small number of schools. Between 400 and 500 schools appear each year in the list of awards made, and among them a number of comparatively small schools whose sixth forms cannot be large.

The next chapter deals with the performance of award-holders after admission. Their performance in GCE A level before admission is significantly better than that of commoners. Eighty-eight per cent of scholars and 76% of exhibitioners with three A levels had scores of 13-15, as against 61% of commoners. This is what might be expected if the two exams are both testing the same general kind of ability; but the figures are worth recording.

5 Performance in university examinations compared with performance in GCE, OES or CJE

The object of those selecting for university admission is to choose candidates who will be successful at the university. Success, it must be remembered, comprises other factors besides the purely academic—for example, the development of personal qualities and of width of interest. But since universities are academic institutions, success in their academic tests in the accepted sense, i.e. in their degree examinations, must have a high and perhaps an overriding importance, and selectors are correspondingly concerned to find a reliable predictor of such success. The instrument used by universities in general is GCE (though Oxford and Cambridge supplement it with their own examinations, as already described); and though A level results are not available for most candidates at most universities when offers are made, it is A level performance that finally decides admission to the universities. Evidence on the relationship between A level performance and subsequent results in university examinations is therefore badly needed. A good deal of work has been done on the problem, but much of it has been limited in scope, and there are no firmly-based conclusions. The consensus of opinion seems to be that A level is the best single predictor at present available, but is by no means uniformly reliable.

It is not clear what basis for comparison should be used. Should single subjects at A level be compared with similar subjects at the university, or should groups of related subjects be treated together? What difference of expectation should there be for subjects studied at both levels (sequential subjects), as against those started for the first time at the university (non-sequential)? What is the effect of a change of subject? In the evidence offered here, the comparison will be between GCE A level scores (calculated on the present accepted basis) and success in winning an award on the one hand, and performance in university examinations on the other. Although evidence for those with two A levels is available, since it does not alter the general picture and three subjects to A level constitute the normal sixth form course (84% of all university entrants had three A levels in 1967), only the scores of candidates with three A levels have been used. A further justification for this basis of comparison is that it represents an estimate of the *whole* of the candidate's achievement in the sixth form course, and that such an overall estimate is arguably the best prognosticator of future performance.

Before the comparative figures are given, certain further qualifications and cautions are necessary. First, the field is already pre-selected; at Oxford and Cambridge, as we have seen, it is highly pre-selected. Those who complain that selection on A level or, at an earlier stage, offers based on O level are only slightly better than decisions on a random basis tend

32

to forget that no university would be willing to accept candidates with no A levels or with O levels below a certain minimum. The field is thus defined, even though further selection within it is indeed often difficult, particularly at the boundaries of choice.

What degree of success should be expected and what standards should be used to measure it? The success of a predictor can be quantified as a correlation coefficient. There is some evidence that even between fairly closely related examinations, such as Parts I and II of a Cambridge Tripos, the correlation coefficient is not more than 0.60 (though D.E. Bagg (see References, p. 46) obtained a figure of 0.67 between Part I and Part II Finals in chemical engineering at the University of Manchester). Between GCE and university examinations the correlation is likely to be much less. Where correlation is far from perfect, it would be unreasonable to expect, for example, that all scholars or high GCE scorers would obtain a high class. The measure used here is that of a comparison between groups, which shows in broad percentage terms whether award-holders and high GCE scorers do better than commoners and low GCE scorers. The judgement is a comparative one—but it makes some estimate of success possible.

Finally, the figures given in the remainder of this chapter are those for men. The smaller numbers of women mean that figures for any one year or subject may not be typical; and if they are added to the figures for men, the result is not materially altered. Where there are noticeable differences, comment is made on them, and two tables giving women's results by GCE score are included as an illustration.

Classes in the university examinations

It is easy to assume that university examinations provide an absolute

Table 11 Percentages of Finals results for men at Oxford (1967 entry): by examination subject and class

Subject	Result				Unfinished*	TOTAL NUMBERS (=100%)
	1	2	3	Pass		
	%	%	%	%	%	
Chemistry	14	56	14	—	16	161
Classics (Greats)	7	53	14	—	26	100
English	8	71	16	1	4	129
History	9	67	18	—	6	249
Jurisprudence	9	66	16	3	6	164
Mathematics	15	51	20	4	10	119
Mod. languages	8	57	22	2	11	158
Physics	12	67	14	2	5	155
PPE	6	67	19	—	8	186

* The percentage unfinished in the Oxford tables is due to the number of four-year courses.

standard. But university examiners are as prone to error as all others, and as a preliminary to the comparison of GCE score and award with university examinations, it is well to look at the actual distribution of classes. The variation between subjects has been commented on in the past and can be seen in Tables 11 and 12.

Table 12 Percentages of Tripos results for men at Cambridge (1967 entry): by examination subject and class

Subject	Part (see p. 45)	Result							TOTAL NUMBERS (=100%)
		1 %	2.1 %	2 %	2.2 %	3 %	Allows %	Other %	
Classics	I	16	36		35	10	3	—	92
	II	19	38		33	9	—	2	58
Economics	I	6	33		44	14	2	2	177
	II	4	33		46	15	1	—	167
Engineering	I	20	24		33	21	2	1	243
	II	8	79		2	1	1	9	90
English	I	10	25		51	12	2	1	181
	II	10	36		46	7	1	1	189
History	I	8	46		37	7	2	—	185
	II	10	50		28	9	1	2	176
Law	I	5	38		35	18	3	—	133
	II	8	39		40	12	2	1	173
Mathematics	I	23		46		29	2	—	254
	II	27		38		31	2	2	184
Mod. languages	I	7	33		41	17	3	—	167
	II	8	33		44	14	1	—	108
Nat. Sciences	I	17	10	30	18	24	2	1	425
	II	16	31		35	17	2	1	486

Nine subjects with a large entry are shown, covering about 80% of the total. Subjects with small numbers are unlikely to be statistically significant. It will be noticed that the proportion of first classes varies at Oxford from 6% to 15% and at Cambridge from 4% to 27%. There are of course variations in other classes too. It is sometimes asked what are the reasons for these differences. Are the proportions right or are they the product as much of custom as of reason? Ideally, they should bear some relation to the ability of candidates. Table 13 shows the relationship between the proportion of award-holders and high GCE scorers reading the subject and the proportion of first classes given. The measure is a rough one, but there is some correspondence. And it is possible to do further calculations. On the basis of the Analysis of Performance for 1966, Dr Dermot Roaf of Exeter College, Oxford, has worked out the average expectation of a first class by GCE score in the nine subjects at Oxford and

Table 13 Rankings for men in nine subjects (1967 entry): by awards, GCE scores and firsts

Subject	Comparative percentages per subject			Subject ranking	
	Scholars & exhibi- tioners	High GCE scores	Firsts	Based on awards & high GCE scores	Based on firsts
	%	%	%		
OXFORD					
Chemistry	48	63	14	3	2
Classics (Greats)	70	65	7	2	8
English	42	37	8	6=	6=
History	34	34	9	9	4=
Jurisprudence	23	37	9	6=	4=
Mathematics	62	66	15	1	1
Mod. languages	42	56	8	5	6=
Physics	45	59	12	4	3
PPE	42	37	6	6=	9
CAMBRIDGE					
Part I					
Nat. sciences	29	79	17	2	3
Classics	51	48	16	3	4
English	31	38	10	6	5
History	29	44	8	7	6
Law	21	41	5	8	9
Mathematics	43	85	23	1	1
Mod. languages	30	58	7	5	7
Engineering	17	73	20	4	2
Economics	14	42	6	9	8
Part II					
Nat. sciences	24	68	16	4	3
Classics	48	43	19	5	2
English	30	37	10	7	4=
History	26	44	10	6	4=
Law	23	41	8	9	6=
Mathematics	51	86	27	1	1
Mod. languages	33	64	8	3	6=
Engineering	30	77	8	2	6=
Economics	17	49	4	8	9

applied it as a standard to each. On this basis, it appears for example that chemistry, mathematics and physics gave rather more than their 'expected' number of firsts, while classics, English and modern languages gave rather less. He has also calculated that on the basis of the total number of those with the different GCE scores accepted by all universities, the number of firsts actually awarded by all universities is some two and a half times more than would be expected on his calculated standard.

The performance of award-holders

The proportion of award-holders placed in the various classes is shown in Tables 14 and 15. The figures call for little comment.

Table 14   Percentages of Finals results for men at Oxford (1967 entry), by award and class

Status	Result				Unfinished	TOTAL NUMBERS (=100%)
	1	2	3	Pass		
	%	%	%	%	%	
Scholars	19	63	8	1	9	422
Exhibitioners	12	63	14	1	10	352
Commoners	5	60	22	2	11	1034
TOTALS	10	61	17	2	10	1808

Table 15   Percentages of Tripos results for men at Cambridge (1967 entry): by award and class

Status	Result						Allows	Other	TOTAL NUMBERS (=100%)
	1	2.1	2	2.2	3		Allows	Other	
	%	%	%	%	%		%	%	
Part I									
Scholars	40	27	14	16	4		1	—	270
Exhibitioners	16	33	16	23	9		2	—	331
Commoners	8	21	9	36	22		3	1	1658
TOTALS	13	24	11	32	18		2	1	2259
Part II									
Scholars	34	37	7	16	5		—	1	244
Exhibitioners	15	39	6	25	14		—	1	300
Commoners	8	32	2	37	17		2	2	1435
TOTALS	12	34	4	32	15		2	2	1979

The performance of award-holders is clearly better than that of commoners, and the two universities can fairly claim that their examinations for entrance and scholarship have a good measure of success in picking

out those likely to produce good degree results. If firsts and upper
seconds at Cambridge are grouped together, a very high proportion of
scholars in the nine subjects listed, in several cases more than 80%, are
placed in the group so formed. It seems fair to generalize further and say
that the examinations are effective selectors over a wider range than that
of the comparatively small fraction constituted by award-holders. How
wide that range may be is a question on which opinions differ: it is commonly held that the examinations are less effective in the lower range of
commoner entry. It is worth noticing here that though the number of
women's awards is proportionally less, women award-holders also do well
(at Oxford rather better than men) and that their examination has always
been used for the dual purpose of award and of commoner entry.

GCE score and university examinations

The relationship between GCE score and university examination results is
shown in Tables 16-19 (pp. 37-9). Again there is little to be added as comment to the figures. They show, in brief, that there is a correspondence
between a high GCE score and a good Finals or Tripos class. The correspondence shows up particularly clearly in the Cambridge results,
where there are figures for two parts of the Tripos and where the second
class is divided. The high scorers have a higher percentage of firsts
and upper seconds, the lower scorers a higher percentage of lower
seconds and thirds.

Neither these figures nor those for award-holders must be inter-
preted to mean more than they say. Individual award-holders and high
scorers may and do obtain a low class; and though the majority of GCE
scorers with a score of ten or less at Cambridge get lower seconds or
thirds, there is a significant minority which gets upper seconds or firsts.
But the general correspondence at both universities is clear enough.

In what has been said above, no account has been taken of the S level
papers. These are, in their nature and intent, an addition to the A level
papers, and they are very difficult to evaluate in terms of a numerical
score. That admissions tutors take them into account has already been

Table 16 Percentages of Finals results for men at Oxford
(1967 entry): by UCCA grade representing GCE score
(see p. 45) and by class

UCCA grade	Result				Unfinished	TOTAL NUMBERS (=100%)
	1	2	3	Pass		
	%	%	%	%	%	
I	14	65	12	1	8	867
II	5	59	22	2	12	549
III	1	50	39	1	9	150

Table 17 Percentages of Tripos results for men at Cambridge (1967 entry): by GCE score and UCCA grade based on three A levels (see p. 45) and by class

GCE score	UCCA grade	Result							TOTAL NUMBERS (=100%)
		1	2.1	2	2.2	3	Allows	Other	
		%	%	%	%	%	%	%	
Part I									
15 ⎫		25	23	23	15	12	2	—	603
14 ⎬	I	13	30	12	29	15	2	—	404
13 ⎭		8	23	8	38	21	3	—	296
12 ⎫		7	24	4	45	18	2	—	232
11 ⎪	II	4	25	3	40	21	5	1	148
10 ⎪		3	21	1	51	20	2	1	108
9 ⎭		—	19	—	52	27	2	—	74
8-3	III	2	16	—	48	30	2	2	87
Part II									
15 ⎫		21	34	10	21	12	1	2	523
14 ⎬	I	15	40	2	27	13	2	2	335
13 ⎭		7	38	1	34	17	2	2	248
12 ⎫		5	34	1	45	12	2	2	199
11 ⎪	II	6	28	1	49	15	1	—	127
10 ⎪		4	38	—	40	17	1	—	95
9 ⎭		3	22	—	48	20	5	3	65
8-3	III	7	17	—	45	29	1	1	73

Table 18 Percentages of Finals results for women at Oxford (1967 entry): by UCCA grade representing GCE score and by class

UCCA grade	Result				Unfinished	TOTAL NUMBERS (=100%)
	1	2	3	Pass		
	%	%	%	%.	%	
I	10	72	14	1	3	244
II	3	73	16	3	5	131
III	—	59	32	—	9	22

noted (p. 14). Statistically it appears that a grade S1 (Distinction) is a fair pointer to subsequent success; at Cambridge some 20% of men with grade S1 get first classes in Part I, some 17% in Part II. Those with grade S2 (Merit) did no better than those with no S grade. In individual cases, much depends on the A level grades with which an S grade is associated, and separate statistical treatment is of limited value.

Table 19 Percentages of Tripos results for women at Cambridge (1967 entry): by GCE score and UCCA grade based on three A levels and by class

GCE score	UCCA grade	Result							TOTAL NUMBERS (= 100%)
		1	2.1	2	2.2	3	Allows	Other	
		%	%	%	%	%	%	%	
Part I									
15 ⎞		18	44	16	16	6	—	—	73
14 ⎬	I	11	37	11	29	11	—	—	35
13 ⎠		—	24	10	45	16	5	—	29
12 ⎞		—	24	15	48	13	—	—	23
11 ⎟	II	4	29	6	38	19	4	—	24
10 ⎟		—	27	3	44	27	—	—	17
9 ⎠		—	43	—	36	—	21	—	7
8-3	III	9	—	9	41	32	9		11
Part II									
15 ⎞		23	49	6	18	5	—	—	66
14 ⎬	I	9	62	—	24	3	3	—	34
13 ⎠		4	39	—	57	—	—	—	23
12 ⎞		9	46	—	41	5	—	—	22
11 ⎟	II	5	53	—	21	21	—	—	19
10 ⎟		6	38	—	38	19	—	—	16
9 ⎠		—	50	—	50	—	—	—	6
8-3	III	11	33	—	44	11	—	—	9

Subjects, boards and schools

From the individual subject tables in the Analysis of Performance for 1966, it is possible to see the distribution of candidates from different boards and types of school between the nine subjects with a large entry. In the case of men, the arts subjects of both universities have a heavy preponderance of candidates from the Oxford and Cambridge Joint Board; in most subjects they number as many as candidates from all other boards put together. An exception is modern languages where, though they still outnumber those from any other single board, the preponderance is not so great. In sciences and mathematics the proportion from other boards is higher, though the Oxford and Cambridge Joint Board contributes the largest number (except in chemistry at Oxford); and as a general rule the London and Joint Matriculation Boards between them provide about the same number of candidates as the Oxford and Cambridge Joint Board. The number of women candidates is too small for any generalization to be made; there are (as already seen) virtually no candidates from the Oxford and Cambridge Joint Board, and candidates from the other four main boards show no particular bias to any field of study.

Women candidates from the three types of school (maintained, direct grant and independent) again show little bias between subjects (other than the general bias against reading science and mathematics noted above, p. 27). But among men the proportion of candidates in arts subjects from the independent schools is considerably larger than that in mathematics and sciences. This does not mean that their numbers in those subjects are small—candidates from the independent and direct grant schools together are comparable in number with those from maintained schools (in engineering considerably more); it is rather that in some arts subjects the numbers from maintained schools are comparatively low. Direct grant school candidates seem fairly evenly spread between subjects.

There is not a great deal of difference between the relative performance of candidates from different boards in Finals and Tripos examinations. The higher proportion of low GCE scorers among the Oxford and Cambridge Joint Board candidates is reflected in a slightly higher proportion of candidates with lower seconds or thirds and a slightly lower proportion of candidates with firsts (see Table 8, p. 26). But even this difference is not large, and in the 1967 entry at Cambridge two boards had a marginally higher proportion of lower seconds and thirds than the Oxford and Cambridge Joint Board. There are, in short, variations both between subjects and between years, but on the evidence so far available no definable trends.

The same is generally true of the results of candidates from the three types of school. The independent school candidates get a slightly smaller proportion of firsts than those from the other two types, and this may again reflect their lower proportion of high GCE scorers. The percentage of firsts obtained by the three types in 1966 and 1967 was: independent about 11%, maintained and direct grant each about 14%. Women obtained a slightly lower percentage of firsts than men, with the independent schools again marginally lower than the others. If firsts and upper seconds at Cambridge are added together, the result for 1967 is as follows:

	Tripos part	Firsts plus upper seconds		
		Maintained %	Direct grant %	Independent %
Men	I	38	41	34
	II	46	48	45
Women	I	42	43	43
	II	60	65	56

It is doubtful how much importance should be attached to these figures, because of the varying distribution of candidates among subjects and the lower percentage of firsts generally given in arts subjects.

6 Conclusion

The purpose of this report has been to present, with brief explanation where needed, facts and figures about the entry to Oxford and Cambridge. The account so presented is best left to speak for itself, but a few brief comments may be made in conclusion.

The greater part of the report consists of a description and analysis of the entry to the two universities and the subsequent performance of the students in university examinations. Any such description needs a proper statistical basis. In future the two universities will publish annually Statistics of Admissions and an Analysis of Performance, in forms that have been agreed. But fresh problems and questions are bound to arise, and the arrangements for the production of statistics should be kept under constant review. It is encouraging to find that in the *Statistical Supplements* to the UCCA *Reports* there are now statistical tables similar to some of those in the Statistics of Admissions for 1970; it has been possible to quote these for comparison in the Statistics of Admissions for 1971.

The college examinations

(a) It appears that there is at present no general desire at either university to discontinue the college examinations or to abolish entrance awards.

(b) The main problem is to ensure that the examinations are suitable for the dual purposes of selecting for admission and making entrance awards, and in particular that the needs of schools which can only run a two-year sixth form course are catered for.

(c) If these needs are met, there is an argument for retaining the examinations as a stabilizing factor at a time when changes in GCE are likely, particularly at sixth form level, though those changes must inevitably be reflected in the college examinations in due course.

(d) There is room for improvement in administrative and procedural arrangements. Such improvement would facilitate consultation and contact with schools.

The composition of the entry

(a) The number of schools sending candidates to the two universities is large and has increased somewhat over the last four years. The number of applications and acceptances from the maintained schools has increased during the same period.

(b) Schools with strong sixth forms have an advantage in competing for places, particularly in view of the entrance standards required.

(c) At a time when the school system is being reorganized, it is desirable to have a rather better classification of school types than the one currently in use, and fuller information about sixth forms. It is hoped to make arrangements for this (see p. 23)

Performance in university examinations

(a) A comparatively high proportion of award-holders obtain a high class in the university examinations, and it is reasonable to suppose that the examinations for entrance and award held by the two universities are effective selectors over a fair range of candidates.

(b) There is a good correspondence between the pattern of GCE scores and the pattern of university examination results, in that the higher scorers are in general found in the higher classes, the lower scorers in the lower. (If a new scheme for grading at A level is introduced, the whole question of scoring A levels will need reconsideration.)

(c) It is possible that we may be reaching the limit of accuracy in prediction by purely academic tests, and that we may need to supplement these by other means, such as tests of relevant non-academic qualities or more carefully structured school reports (there is some evidence from St John's College, Cambridge, that school reports can be used in this way).

The figures make it plain that in terms of A level achievement the quality of the Oxford and Cambridge entrance is high. Some overall comparisons in this and other respects are made possible by the *Statistical Supplements* to the UCCA *Reports* in their present form. But what would figures comparable to those given here show if they were available for other universities individually? And to what conclusions would they lead? Perhaps the questions have awkward implications. But consideration of the structure of university and higher education is better based on knowledge than on guesswork, and it has been the object of this report to supply that knowledge, at least in some measure, for two universities.

Appendix

A trial run with the data for the Cambridge 1971 entry (made with the help of the Department of Education and Science, as mentioned on p. 23) gives the following result for sixth form sizes, which can be compared with Table 5 on p 23.

Table 5a Numbers of schools of different sixth form size sending applicants (A) and securing places (P), compared with all schools

Sixth form size	Boys' schools			Mixed schools			Girls' schools		
	Cambridge A	P	All	Cambridge A	P	All	Cambridge A	P	All
1-90:									
no. of schools	117	73	385	148	58	978	161	49	614
%	22	17	44	36	26	70	40	30	64
91-120:									
no. of schools	101	76	119	70	45	146	93	40	167
%	19	17	14	17	20	10	24	24	17
121-150:									
no. of schools	123	105	140	70	41	112	79	34	105
%	23	24	16	17	18	8	20	21	11
151-210:									
no. of schools	133	116	143	63	47	113	56	33	65
%	24	27	16	20	21	8	14	20	7
211 and over:									
no. of schools	68	68	69	75	54	93	11	7	12
%	12	15	8	10	15	3	2	4	1
TOTALS:									
no. of schools	542	438	856	426	245	1442	400	163	963
%	100	100	100	100	100	100	100	100	100

The same trial run gave the following figures for applications and acceptances from comprehensive schools:

	Men	Women
Applications		
No. from comprehensive schools (England and Wales)	386	137
No. from comprehensive schools as percentage of total from all schools (England and Wales)	*8.8*	*8.7*
*Acceptances**		
No. from comprehensive schools (England and Wales)	170	28
No. from comprehensive schools as percentage of total from all schools (England and Wales)	*7.7*	*8.3*

* Some 49% of all men applicants and 20% of all women applicants are accepted (see Table 3, p. 21).

Notes to tables

Figures available

The figures given in the tables are those for the latest year available, and may be taken as typical. Figures for admissions are available for the years 1966-71; those for performance are available for the entries of 1966 and 1967 (see References, p. 46). Figures for the 1970 or 1971 admissions relate to the position before the summer GCE results are available and so the number of acceptances does not correspond exactly to the number who actually began their course in the following October. The performance figures for the Cambridge 1967 entry do not include those who took their final examination in 1971.

Tripos result at Cambridge

At Cambridge the Tripos results have been listed under Part I and Part II. In general this refers to the first and second part of a Tripos. Exceptions are classified along the following general lines. Where the first part of a Tripos examination is split, the two first parts are each counted as half of Part I for that particular candidate; similarly, where a candidate has taken the second and third parts of a Tripos, or two second parts, these are each counted as half of Part II. Where a candidate has taken the first part a Tripos, and then completed his degree by taking the first part of another Tripos, the second Tripos examination is counted as a Part II.

UCCA grades and GCE scores

The GCE score is calculated on three A levels—or the best three where more than three were taken—or on two A levels, by adding together the score for each A level pass: $A = 5, B = 4, C = 3, D = 2, E = 1$. GCE scores are grouped by UCCA in grades as follows:

UCCA grade	Three or more A levels	Two A levels
I	15-13	10-9
II	12-9	8-6
III	8-3	5-2

References

University publications

Statistics of Admissions
1970: *Oxford University Gazette,* 5 August 1970, Supplement (2).
 Cambridge University Reporter, 1 July 1970.
1971: *Oxford University Gazette,* 26 January 1972.
 Cambridge University Reporter, 21 July 1971.

Analysis of Performance
1967 entry: *Oxford University Gazette,* (to be published summer 1972;
 now in duplicated form from Oxford Admissions Office)
 Cambridge University Reporter, 6 October 1971.

Cambridge entry examination
Working Party on the Cambridge Colleges' Joint Examination. *First
 Report* and *Second Report.* Cambridge Intercollegiate Applications
 Office, November 1970 and November 1971.

Publications from the project

(Available from the Oxford Admissions Office or the Cambridge Intercollegiate Applications Office)

*A Survey of Information on Admissions and Awards at Oxford and Cam-
 bridge.* July 1969.
*Analysis of the 1966 Oxford and Cambridge Entry by GCE, Award and
 Degree Result.* January 1971.

Other publications

Ashby, Sir Eric. *Technology and the Academics.* Macmillan, 1970.
Bagg, D. E. 'A-levels and university performance', *Nature,* **225,** no. 5328,
 21 March 1970.
Committee of Vice-Chancellors and Principals of the Universities of the
 United Kingdom. *A Compendium of University Entrance Requirements
 for First Degree Courses in the United Kingdom in 1969-70.* Associa-
 tion of Commonwealth Universities, 1968.
Department of Education and Science. *Statistics of Education, 1969,* vol. 1,
 Schools. HMSO, 1970.
Headmasters' Association. *HMA Review,* December 1969 and July 1971.
Kelsall, R. K. *Report on an Inquiry into Applications for Admission to
 Universities.* Association of Commonwealth Universities, 1957.
Miller, G. W. *Success, Failure and Wastage in Higher Education.* Harrap,
 1970.

Reid, A. W. *The Universities and the Sixth Form Curriculum (Schools Council Research Studies)*. Macmillan Education (distributor), 1972.

Universities Central Council on Admissions. *Statistical Supplement to the Seventh Report, 1968/9* and *to the Eighth Report, 1969/70*.*

> *   The *Supplement to the Eighth Report* appeared when this project's report was already in final draft form. The overall picture it presents does not differ greatly from that of the *Seventh Report*. The figures in Tables 1, 3 and 7 are those of the *Eighth Report*.

University of Oxford: Report of Commission of Inquiry [Franks Report]. 2 vols, Oxford University Press, 1966.

Welford, A. T. *Research on Admissions*. Cambridge: St John's College, 1971.